CHÂTEAU-MYSTÈRE
MYSTERY CASTLE

Illustrated by Brenda Haw

Adapted from Puzzle Castle, in the Usborne Young Puzzles series, by
Kathy Gemmell

Bilingual editor: Nicole Irving
Design adaptation by John Russell
Language consultant: Lorraine Sharp

Original story by Susannah Leigh
Edited by Gaby Waters
Designed by Paul Greenleaf

Contents

About this book

This book is about a brave knight called Sophie and her adventure at Mystery Castle. The story is in French and English. You can look up the word list on page 23 if you want to check what any French word means. This list also shows you how to say each French word.

Château-Mystère

Sophie

There is a puzzle on every double page. Solve each one and help Sophie on her way. All the French words you need to solve the puzzles are in the word keys (look out for this sign: 🔑). If you get stuck, the answers are on page 22.

L'histoire The story

L'ami de Sophie, Simon, habite le Château-Mystère. Il lui a écrit cette lettre:

Sophie's friend, Simon, lives in Mystery Castle. He has written her this letter:

Simon

Château-Mystère	Mystery Castle
Chère Sophie,	Dear Sophie,
Tu es invitée, ce soir, au banquet du château.	You are invited to the castle banquet this evening.
Il commencera à six heures.	It will start at six.
Nous avons un petit problème.	We have a little problem.
Il y a un monstre quelque part dans les oubliettes.	There is a monster somewhere in the dungeons.
Tu es très, très, très courageuse.	You are very, very, very brave.
Peux-tu venir en avance pour trouver le monstre?	Can you come early and find the monster?
Ton ami, Simon	Your friend, Simon

Things to look for

When Sophie gets to the castle, she must collect the seven things shown here. They will all help her to find the monster. You will find one of them on each double page, from the moment she sees the castle, until she reaches the dungeons.

le parapluie vert
green umbrella

la lampe de poche extra-puissante
extra-powerful flashlight

les chaussures-vitesse
run-fast shoes

le bouclier anti-monstre
anti-monster shield

le dictionnaire du langage monstre
monster-language dictionary

le casque anti-monstre
anti-monster helmet

la clé
key

Thomas, the ghost

Mystery Castle is haunted by a friendly ghost, called Thomas. He is hiding on every double page. See if you can spot him.

Jim, the juggler

Jim is working on his juggling for the banquet, but he is not very good at it. He has lost his juggling balls around the castle. There is at least one hiding on every double page. Can you find them?

The juggling balls look like this.

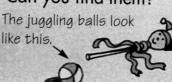

How to sound French

Here are a few tips to help you say French sounds and letters in a French way.

The letter à is said like the "a" in "cat", â like the "a" in "part", ai, è, and ê like the "e" in "sell", é like the "a" in "late" and i like the "i" in "machine". You often say the French e and eu like the "u" in "fur". To say u, round your lips as if to say "oo", then try to say "ee". Say au and eau like the "o" in "rose" and oi like the "wa" in "wagon".

You never say h and you do not usually say s, t or r at the end of a word; n is often said like the "n" in "aunt", ch sounds like the "sh" in "show" and j sounds like the "s" in "measure". The French r is rolled at the back of your mouth, a little like gargling.

3

Le château   The castle

Sophie se met tout de suite en route pour le château.
Sophie sets off for the castle at once.

Elle dit au revoir à ses parents.
She says goodbye to her parents.

Elle arrive bientôt aux douves du château.
Soon she arrives at the castle moat.

Mais quel chemin doit-elle prendre pour traverser?
But which route must she take to cross?

Le lapin lui donne la première indication.
The rabbit gives her the first direction.

Can you spot the rabbit?
Follow all the directions and find the right
way to cross the moat.

Le plan The map

Sophie trouve Simon devant le hall du château. Il lui donne un plan du château.

Sophie finds Simon outside the castle entrance hall. He gives her a map of the castle.

"Le monstre est dans les oubliettes. Pour y arriver, tu dois aller à la cave."

"The monster is in the dungeons. To get there, you have to go to the cellar."

"En chemin, tu dois rendre visite à quatre personnes."

"On the way, you must visit four people."

"Tout le monde se prépare pour le banquet. Chaque personne a besoin de ton aide."

"Everybody is getting ready for the banquet. Each person needs your help."

Can you match the four people on the list with the rooms where Sophie will find them? She must visit them in order. Which route will she take to the cellar?

Sophie doit trouver:
Sophie must find:

1. Justin, le gardien des portraits
Justin, the portrait keeper

2. La princesse Fleur
Princess Fleur

3. Eric, le guetteur
Eric, the look-out boy

4. Madame Croûton, la cuisinière
Mrs. Croûton, the cook

Key 🔑

la tour de guet	look-out tower
le grenier	attic
le bureau	study
la chambre de...	...'s bedroom
la galerie des portraits	portrait gallery
le hall	entrance hall
les oubliettes	dungeons
la grande salle	banquet hall
la cuisine	kitchen
la salle de bain	bathroom
l'escalier	stairs
la cave	cellar
le garage	garage
la bibliothèque	library

Plan du château Map of the castle

la tour de guet

le grenier

le bureau

la chambre de Simon

la chambre de Fleur

la bibliothèque

la galerie des portraits

la grande salle

la salle de bain

le hall

la cuisine

l'escalier

le garage

la cave

les oubliettes

La galerie des portraits
The portrait gallery

Sophie visite d'abord la galerie des portraits.
Sophie's first visit is to the portrait gallery.

Justin, le gardien des portraits, est inquiet.
Justin, the portrait keeper, is worried.

"Oncle Stan vient au banquet."
"Uncle Stan is coming to the banquet."

"Je dois le rencontrer près des douves, mais j'ai oublié comment il est."
"I have to meet him by the moat, but I've forgotten what he looks like."

Which portrait is Uncle Stan's? There is only one which fits what everyone is saying.

Key

il a	he has
il n'a pas de/d'	he does not have a (OR any)
il s'habille	he dresses
il porte	he has (he wears)
les cheveux noirs	black hair
une moustache	a moustache
(les) enfants	children
(le) cheval	horse
une barbe	a beard
rouge	red
violet	purple
toujours	always
en	in
et	and

Il porte
une barbe.

Il n'a pas
de cheval.

9

La chasse au trésor
The treasure hunt

Ensuite, Sophie rend visite à la princesse Fleur.
Next, Sophie visits Princess Fleur.

Elle est dans sa chambre. Quel désordre!
She is in her bedroom. What a mess!

"Te voilà, Sophie!" crie Fleur.
"There you are, Sophie!" shouts Fleur.

"J'ai perdu mon collier, mon bracelet, ma bague et
ma couronne."
"I've lost my necklace, my bracelet, my ring and my crown."

Plusieurs autres choses ont disparu.
Several other things have disappeared.

**Can you find a necklace, bracelet, ring and crown
that match? Read the speech bubbles and point
to all the other things that are lost.**

10

La tour de guet   The look-out tower

Sophie quitte la princesse. Elle monte à la tour de guet.
Des gens arrivent déjà pour le banquet.
Sophie leaves the princess. She climbs up to the look-out tower.
People are already arriving for the banquet.

Eric, le guetteur, ne sait pas si tout le monde est invité.
"Sophie," crie-t-il, "fais quelque chose!"
Eric, the look-out boy, does not know if everyone is invited.
"Sophie," he cries, "do something!"

**Using Eric's list, can you help Sophie tell him which of
the people in the picture are not invited? What
treatment will they get?**

La liste d'Eric

La reine de Jonville, Juliette: invitée.
La reine de Montfort, Marianne: pas invitée -
traitement au fumier.
La princesse de Gouache, Géraldine: invitée.
La reine de Gaumont, Géraldine: pas invitée -
traitement à la soupe à l'oignon.
La reine de Beaufort, Béatrice: pas invitée -
traitement à la confiture.
Le roi de Roquefort, Roland: invité.
Le prince de Roquefort, Boris, et son chien, Fang:
pas invités - traitement aux oeufs pourris.

OEUFS POURRIS

FUMIER

CONFITURE   SOUPE À L'OIGNON

Key 🔑

je m'appelle	my name is	(le) traitement au/à la/aux	treatment
je viens de	I come from		
la liste	list	(les) oeufs pourris	rotten eggs
le roi	king	(le) fumier	dung
la reine	queen	(la) soupe à l'oignon	onion soup
le prince	prince	(la) confiture	jam
la princesse	princess	son chien	his dog
invité(e)	invited	de/d'/des	of
pas invité(e)(s)	not invited	et	and

13

Dans la cuisine In the kitchen

Ensuite, Sophie va à la cuisine.
Next, Sophie goes to the kitchen.

Madame Croûton a l'air inquiet.
Mrs. Croûton looks worried.

"Qu'est-ce qu'il y a?" demande Sophie.
"What's the matter?" asks Sophie.

"Je dois faire un grand gâteau pour le banquet, mais je ne trouve pas tous les ingrédients.
"I must bake a big cake for the banquet, but I can't find all the ingredients."

"Je sais qu'ils sont ici quelque part."
"I know they're here somewhere".

Can you spot all the ingredients Mrs. Croûton is looking for somewhere in the kitchen?

Key

je cherche	I am looking for
un	one OR a
deux	two
trois	three
quatre	four
un pot de	a pot of
(le) miel	honey
(les) oeufs	eggs
(les) pains	loaves of bread
(le) citron	lemon
(les) prunes rouges	red plums
(le) sucre	sugar
(la) farine	flour
(le) fromage	cheese
(le) lait	milk
(l') eau	water
frais	fresh
et	and

Je cherche deux prunes rouges, un pot de miel, trois oeufs frais, quatre pains et un citron.

La cave The cellar

Sophie quitte la cuisine et descend dans la cave.
Sophie leaves the kitchen and goes down to the cellar.

"Oh," dit-elle, en regardant le plan, "il y a beaucoup de portes ici."
"Oh," she says, looking at the map, "there are lots of doors here."

"Quelle est la bonne porte pour aller aux oubliettes?"
"Which is the right door to get to the dungeons?"

Heureusement pour Sophie, les animaux qui habitent la cave disent toujours la vérité.
Luckily for Sophie, the animals who live in the cellar always tell the truth.

Can you work out from what all the animals are saying which door Sophie should take?

16

17

Dans les oubliettes In the dungeons

Enfin, Sophie entre dans les oubliettes.
At last, Sophie enters the dungeons.

Elle entend des voix bizarres.
She hears strange voices.

"Simon m'a prévenue," dit-elle.
"Simon warned me about this," she says.

"Les animaux qui habitent ici ne disent jamais la vérité."
"The animals who live here never tell the truth."

"Je dois toujours faire le contraire de ce qu'ils disent."
"I must always do the opposite of what they say."

Read what the animals are saying. Can you give Sophie the correct directions to find the monster?

Did you remember to look for all Sophie's useful equipment? Look back to page 3 to check you have found everything.

Key 🔑

ouvre	open
n'ouvre pas	do not open
la porte	the door
tourne	turn
ne tourne pas	do not turn
à droite	right
à gauche	left
comment tu t'appelles?	what is your name?
je m'appelle	my name is
j'ai perdu	I have lost
ma maman	my mom
la clé	the key

Le banquet   The banquet

C'est l'heure du banquet.
It is time for the banquet.

Sophie et le petit monstre s'amusent bien. Les vois-tu?
Sophie and the little monster are having a great time.
Can you see them?

Tout le monde est très content, mais plusieurs invités ont perdu des choses.
Everyone is very happy, but several guests have lost things.

Sophie ne peut pas tous les aider.
Sophie cannot help them all.

Can you spot all the things that people are looking for? Who will be especially pleased to see the little monster?

Answers

Pages 4-5

The route Sophie should take is shown in red.

Pages 6-7

Sophie's route will take her to: Justin in la galerie des portraits (the portrait gallery), Fleur in la chambre de Fleur (Fleur's bedroom), Eric in la tour de guet (the look-out tower) and Mrs. Croûton in la cuisine (the kitchen).

Pages 8-9

This is Uncle Stan's portrait.

Pages 10-11

Fleur's matching jewels are circled in red. All the other missing objects are circled in blue.

Pages 12-13

Boris, le prince de Roquefort and his dog, Fang are not invited. They will get the rotten egg treatment.

Pages 14-15

The missing ingredients are circled in red.

Pages 16-17

Sophie should go through this door.

Pages 18-19

Here are the correct directions: Tourne à gauche. Tourne à droite. Tourne à gauche. Tourne la clé. Ouvre la porte.

The monster is crying because he has lost his mom.

Pages 20-21

All the things that people are looking for are circled in red. Sniff's mom is especially pleased to see him. Here she is.

Did you spot everything?

Pages	Juggling balls	Equipment to find
4-5	one	anti-monster shield
6-7	one	key
8-9	three	extra-powerful flashlight
10-11	four	run-fast shoes
12-13	two	green umbrella
14-15	four	monster-language dictionary
16-17	two	anti-monster helmet
18-19	one	none here!
20-21	nineteen	none here!

Did you remember to look out for Thomas the ghost? Look back and find him on every double page.

Word list and pronunciation guide

Here is a list of all the French words and phrases used in this book. All the naming words (nouns) have le, la, l' or les before them. These all mean "the". In French, all nouns are either masculine or feminine. You use le with masculine nouns and la with feminine nouns; l' or les nouns have [m] or [f] after them to show if they are masculine or feminine. When you see les, it means the noun is plural (more than one).

Some French describing words (adjectives) change when they describe feminine nouns. Here, the masculine version is written first, followed by the feminine word. When an adjective describes a plural noun, it usually has an "s" on the end, for example: les prunes rouges (red plums).

Each French word in this list has its pronunciation shown after it (in letters like this). Read these pronunciation letters as if they were English words. You will sometimes see (n) or (m), which you should say slightly through your nose, as if you had a cold. You can read more about how to say French words on page 3.

à	ah	to
...a besoin	ah buhzwa(n)	...needs
à droite	ah drwat	(to the) right
à gauche	ah gawsh	(to the) left
l'aide [f]	led	help
aider	edday	to help
...a l'air	ah lair	...seems OR looks
aller	alay	to go
l'ami [m]	lamee	friend
les animaux [m]	laiz aneemo	animals
arriver	areevay	to arrive
au, à la, à l', aux	oh, ah la, ah l, oh	to the OR at the
au revoir	oh ruh vwar	goodbye
au secours	oh suhkoor	help
aussi	ohsee	also
autre	ohtr	other
avec	avek	with
la bague	la bag	ring
le banquet	luh bo(n)kay	banquet
la barbe	la barb	beard
beaucoup	bokoo	a lot
la bibliothèque	la beebly otek	library
bientôt	bee a(n)toh	soon
bienvenue	bee a(n)vuhnew	welcome
bizarre	beezar	strange
bleu, bleue	bluh	blue
bon, bonne	bo(n), bonn	good
bonjour	bo(n)joor	hello
le bouclier	luh booklee ay	shield
le bracelet	luh brasslay	bracelet
le bureau	luh bewro	study
le casque	luh kask	helmet
la cave	la kav	cellar
ce, cette	suh, set	this
c'est	sai	it is
la chambre	la sho(m)br	bedroom
chaque	shak	each
la chasse au trésor	la shass oh traizor	treasure hunt
le chat	luh sha	cat
le château	luh shatoh	castle
les chaussures [f]	lay show sewr	shoes
le chemin	luh shuhma(n)	way OR path
cher, chère	sher, shair	dear
le cheval	luh shuhval	horse
les cheveux [m]	lay shuhvuh	hair
le chien	luh shee a(n)	dog
les choses [f]	lay shoz	things
cinq	sa(n)k	five
le citron	luh seetro(n)	lemon
la clé	la klay	key
le cochon	luh kosho(n)	pig
le collier	luh kollee ay	necklace
comment il est	kommo(n) eel ai	what he looks like
comment tu t'appelles?	kommo(n) tew tapell	what is your name?
la confiture	la ko(n)feetewr	jam
content, contente	ko(n)to(n), ko(n)to(n)t	happy
le contraire	luh ko(n)trair	opposite
le cor	luh kor	horn
courageux, courageuse	koorashuh, koorashuhz	brave
la couronne	la kooronn	crown
...crie	kree	...shouts
le croûton	luh krooto(n)	crouton
la cuisine	la kweezeen	kitchen
la cuisinière	la kweezeen yair	cook
d'abord	dabor	first
dans	do(n)	in
de	duh	of
déjà	daysha	already
...demande	duhmo(n)d	...asks
...descend	desso(n)	...goes down
deux	duh	two
devant	duhvo(n)	in front of
le dictionnaire	luh deeks yonair	dictionary
dit-elle	deet el	she says
doit-elle	dwat el	must she
...donne	don	...gives
les douves [f]	lay doov	moat
du, de la, de l', des	dew, duh la, duh l, day	of the
l'eau [f]	loh	water
elle	el	she, it

elle arrive	el areev	she arrives
elle dit	el dee	she says
elle doit	el dwa	she must
elle entend	el o(n)to(n)	she hears
elle monte	el mo(n)t	she climbs
elle regarde	el ruhgard	she looks
en	o(n)	in
en avance	o(n) avo(n)ss	early
en chemin	o(n) shuhma(n)	on the way
en regardant	o(n) ruhgardo(n)	looking
les enfants [m]	laiz o(n)fo(n)	children
enfin	o(n)fa(n)	at last
ensuite	o(n)sweet	next, then
...entre (dans)	o(n)tr (do(n))	...enters
l'escalier [m]	lesskal yay	stairs
...est	ai	...is
et	ay	and
faire	fair	to do OR to make
fais	fai	do
la farine [f]	la fareen	flour
le fils	luh feess	son
les fleurs [f]	lay flur	flowers
la flûte (à bec)	la flewt (ah bek)	recorder
frais, fraîche	frai, fraish	fresh
le fromage	luh fromajsh	cheese
le fumier	luh fewm yay	dung
la galerie des portraits	la galree day portrai	portrait gallery
le garage	luh garajsh	garage
le gardien	luh gardee a(n)	keeper
le gâteau	luh gatoh	cake
les gens [m/f]	lay sho(n)	people
gentil, gentille	sho(n)tee, sho(n)teey	nice
grand, grande	gro(n), gro(n)d	big
la grande salle	la gro(n)d sal	banquet hall
le grenier	luh gruhnee ay	attic
le guetteur	luh gettuhr	look-out boy
...habite	abeet	...lives in
le hall	luh al	entrance hall
l'heure [f]	luhr	time
...heures [f]	uhr	...o'clock
heureusement	uhruhzmo(n)	luckily
l'histoire [f]	leesstwar	story
ici	eessee	here
il	eel	he, it
il a	eel a	he has
il a écrit	eel a aikree	he has written
il commencera	eel kommo(n)suhra	it will start
il est	eel ai	he is
il n'a pas de/d'	eel na pa duh/d	he does not have a (OR any)
il porte	eel port	he has OR he wears OR he carries
ils arrivent	eelzareev	they arrive

ils disent	eel deez	they say
il s'habille	eel sabeey	he dresses
ils sont	eel so(n)	they are
il y a	eel ee a	there is OR there are
l'indication [f]	la(n)deekassee o(n)	direction
les ingrédients [m]	laiz a(n)graidee o(n)	ingredients
inquiet, inquiète	a(n)kee ai, a(n)k yet	worried
invité, invitée	a(n)veetai	invited
les invités [m]	laiz a(n)veetai	guests
j'ai oublié	shai ooblee yai	I have forgotten
j'ai perdu	shai perdew	I have lost
jamais	shamai	never
jaune	shone	yellow
je	shuh	I
je cherche	shuh shersh	I am looking for
je dois	shuh dwa	I must
je m'appelle	shuh mapell	my name is OR I am called
je ne trouve pas	shuh nuh troov pa	I cannot find
je sais	shuh sai	I know
je viens de	shuh vee a(n) duh	I come from
le lait	luh lai	milk
la lampe de poche	la lo(m)p de posh	flashlight
le langage	luh lo(n)gajsh	language
le lapin	luh lapa(n)	rabbit
le, la, l', les	luh, la, l, lay	the
la lettre	la letr	letter
la liste	la leest	list
lui	lwee	to him OR to her
les lunettes [f]	lay lewnett	glasses
mais	mai	but
la maman	la mamo(n)	mom
...m'a prévenu(e)	ma praivuhnew	...warned me
...met	mai	...puts on
le miel	luh meeyell	honey
mon, ma, mes	mo(n), ma, may	my
le monstre	luh mo(n)str	monster
la montre	la mo(n)tr	watch
la moustache	la mooss tash	moustache
le mystère	luh meess tair	mystery
...ne peut pas	nuh puh pas	...cannot
ne prends pas	nuh pro(n) pa	do not take
...ne sait pas	nuh sai pa	...does not know
ne tourne pas	nuh toorn pa	do not turn
noir, noire	nwar	black
le nounours	luh noonoorss	teddy bear
nous avons	noozavo(n)	we have
n'ouvre pas	noovruh pa	don't open
le numéro	luh newmairo	number
les oeufs [m]	laiz uh	eggs
l'oignon [m]	lonn yo(n)	onion
l'oncle [m]	lo(n)kl	uncle

24

...ont disparu	o(n) deesparew	...have disappeared		le roi	luh rwa	king
...ont perdu	o(n) perdew	...have lost		rouge	roojsh	red
orange	oro(n)sh	orange				
les oubliettes [f]	laiz ooblee ett	dungeons		la salle de bain	la sal duh ba(n)	bathroom
où est..?	oo ai	where is...?		...s'amusent bien	sa mewz bee a(n)	...are having a great time
ouvre (la porte)	oovr (la port)	open (the door)				
				...se met en route	suh met o(n) root	...sets off
le pain	luh pa	bread		...se prépare	suh praipar	...is getting ready
les pains [m]	lay pa	loaves of bread		si	see	if
le parapluie	luh para plwee	umbrella		six	seess	six
les parents [m]	lay paro(n)	parents		le soir	luh swar	evening
pas invité, pas invitée	paza(n)veetai	not invited		son, sa, ses	so(n), sa, say	his OR her
				la soupe	la soop	soup
passage interdit	passajsh a(n)terdee	no entry		la souris	la sooree	mouse
la personne	la personn	person		le sucre	luh sewkr	sugar
petit, petite	puhtee, puhteet	little				
peux-tu ..?	puh tew	can you...?		te voilà	tuh vwala	there you are
le plan	luh plo(n)	map		ton, ta, tes	to(n), ta, tay	your
plusieurs	plewz yuhr	several		toujours	tooshoor	always
le pont	luh po(n)	bridge		la tour de guet	la toor duh gai	look-out tower
la porte	la port	door		tourne	toorn	turn
le pot	luh po	pot		tous	tooss	all
pour	poor	for OR in order to		tout de suite	too duh sweet	at once
pourri, pourrie	pooree	rotten		tout droit	too drwa	straight ahead
premier, première	prem yai, prem yair	first		tout le monde	too luh mo(n)d	everyone
prendre	pro(n)dr	to take		le traitement	luh tretmo(n)	treatment
prends	pro(n)	take		traverser	traversay	to cross
près	prai	near		très	trai	very
le prince	luh pra(n)ss	prince		trois	trwa	three
la princesse	la pra(n)sess	princess		...trouve	troov	...finds
le problème	luh problaim	problem		trouver	troovay	to find
les prunes [f]	lay prewn	plums		tu dois	tew dwa	you must
puissant puissante	pweesso(n), pweesso(n)t	powerful		tu es	tew ai	you are
				un, une	a(n), ewn	one OR a
quatre	katr	four				
que, qu'	kuh, k	that		va	va	go
quelle	kel	which OR what		venir	vuhneer	to come
quel désordre	kel daizordr	what a mess		la vérité	la vaireetai	truth
quelque chose	kelkuh shoz	something		vert, verte	vair, vairt	green
quelque part	kelkuh par	somewhere		...vient	vee a(n)	...comes
qu'est-ce qu'il y a?	kess keel ee a	what is the matter?		violet, violette	vee olay, vee olet	purple
...quitte	keet	...leaves		...visite	veezeet	...visits (a place)
				la vitesse	la veetess	speed
la reine	la ren	queen		vois-tu ..?	vwa tew	can you see...?
rencontrer	ro(n)ko(n)tray	to meet		la voix	la vwa	voice
rendre visite à	ro(n)dr veezeet ah	to visit (a person)				
...rend visite à	ro(n) veezeet ah	...visits		y	ee	there

This bilingual edition first published in 1994 by Usborne Publishing Ltd., Usborne House, 83-85 Saffron Hill, London EC1N 8RT. Based on a previous title first published in 1992.

Copyright © 1994, 1992 Usborne Publishing Ltd.

Printed in Portugal. First published in America March 1995. AE